EXPLORE THE WRLD

SOCIAL SCIENCE

Jane Goodall

TRINA LAWRENCE

TABLE OF CONTENTS

PIONEER VALLEY EDUCATIONAL PRESS, INC

WHO IS JANE GOODALL?

Jane Goodall studied chimpanzees

for many years.

She has helped us learn

new things about these animals.

3

JANE'S EARLY LIFE

When Jane was a little girl,

she was interested in animals

and how they **behave**.

She liked to watch birds and other animals.

She would draw pictures

and read books about animals.

A TRIP TO AFRICA

In 1957, Jane went to Africa to visit a friend's farm. She worked for a **scientist** who studied **wild** chimpanzees. She became very interested in chimpanzees.

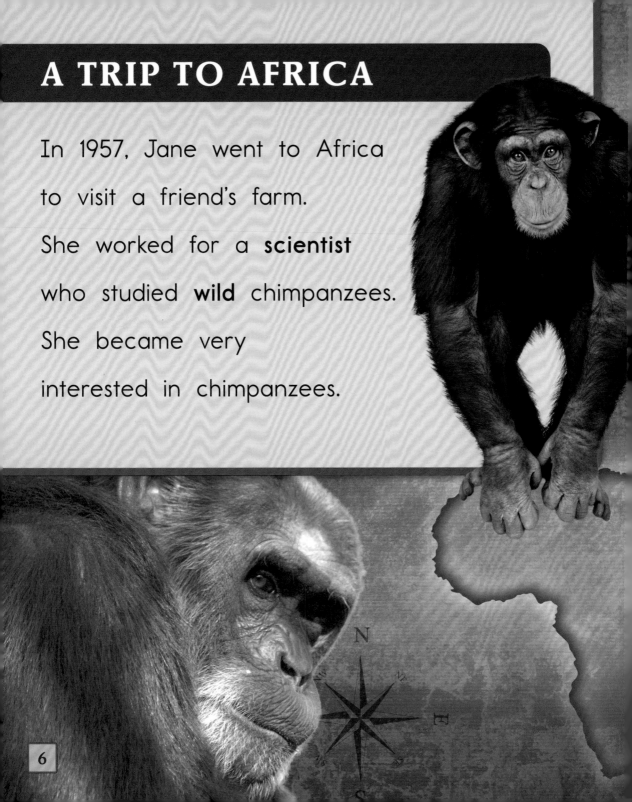

Jane went back home to go to school.
At school, she learned about chimpanzees
and other kinds of monkeys.

In 1960, Jane went back to Africa.
She set up a camp near a place
where there were lots of chimpanzees.
She began to watch them.

STUDYING CHIMPANZEES

At first, when Jane went near

the chimpanzees,

they would run away.

They were afraid of people.

Every morning, Jane would

sit near the chimpanzees' feeding place.

She would offer them bananas.

After a long time,

the chimpanzees let Jane

get closer and closer.

Jane learned many things
about chimpanzees.

Jane watched how chimpanzees would

catch termites for food.

Chimpanzees would take blades of grass

and put them into **termite** hills.

Then they would pull the blades out

and the blades of grass

would have termites on them.

The chimpanzees would use the blades

of grass like a spoon to eat the termites!

11

This was exciting to find out.
Jane also saw the chimpanzees
using other kinds of tools.
At the time, people believed
only **humans** used tools.

Chimpanzees use rocks to smash open nuts. They also use leaves to soak up water to drink.

MORE TO EXPLORE

13

Jane learned that chimpanzees
can be happy or sad.
She saw chimpanzees giving kisses,
hugs, and pats on the back
to each other.

Chimps laugh when they are tickled.

People thought chimpanzees
only ate plants and fruit,
but Jane found out this was not true.
She saw them eating eggs and insects.
She watched the chimpanzees
catch and eat small monkeys.

HELPING ANIMALS

Some scientists hurt animals
when they are studying them.
Jane has helped people understand
that chimpanzees
should not be treated badly.
She believes scientists
need to work harder
to find ways to study
chimpanzees and other animals
without hurting them.

TIONAL PRESS CLUB

Jane made movies

and wrote books about chimpanzees.

She helped people

learn about wild chimpanzees

and their **habitat.**

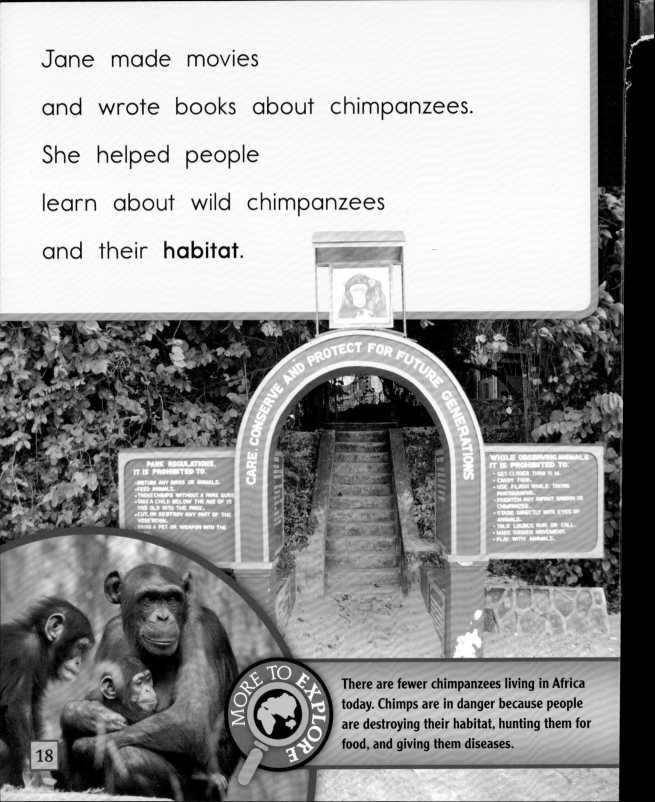

PARK REGULATIONS.
IT IS PROHIBITED TO:

- DISTURB ANY BIRDS OR ANIMALS.
- FEED ANIMALS.
- TREKK CHIMPS WITHOUT A PARK GUIDE.
- TAKE A CHILD BELOW THE AGE OF 15 YRS OLD INTO THE PARK.
- CUT, OR DESTROY ANY PART OF THE VEGETATION.
- BRING A PET OR WEAPON INTO THE

CARE, CONSERVE AND PROTECT FOR FUTURE GENERATIONS

WHILE OBSERVING ANIMALS
IT IS PROHIBITED TO:

- GET CLOSER THAN 10 M.
- CARRY FOOD.
- USE FLASH WHILE TAKING PHOTOGRAPHS.
- FRIGHTEN ANY INFANT BABOON OR CHIMPANZEE.
- STARE DIRECTLY INTO EYES OF ANIMALS.
- TALK LOUDLY, RUN OR CALL.
- MAKE SUDDEN MOVEMENT.
- PLAY WITH ANIMALS.

MORE TO EXPLORE

There are fewer chimpanzees living in Africa today. Chimps are in danger because people are destroying their habitat, hunting them for food, and giving them diseases.

Jane has helped people in Africa make safe places for visitors to see the chimpanzees.

Jane has been given many awards for all her work.

珍古道尔（北京）环境文化交流中心
the Jane Goodall Institute China

.1

1965

Jane earns a PhD in ethology
(the study of animal behavior).

1977

Jane founds the Jane Goodall
Institute for Wildlife Research,
Education, and Conservation.

2002

Jane is named a United Nations
Messenger of Peace.

2015

Jane continues her work,
speaking around the world about
the threats against chimpanzees.

珍古道尔（北京）环境文化交流中心
the Jane Goodall Institute China

Jane Goodal

TIME LINE

1934
Jane is born on April 3.

1952
Jane graduates from high school and becomes a secretary.

1956
Jane is invited to a friend's house in Africa.

1960
Jane begins to study chimpanzees.

1961
Jane discovers chimpanzees using tools.

GLOSSARY

behave
how you act

habitat
the place where a plant
grows or an animal lives

humans
people

scientist
a person who is trained
in science

termite
a soft, white insect that
eats wood

wild
living in a place where
there are no people

INDEX

20